PARENTING WITHOUT BORDERS

PARENTING WITHOUT BORDERS

LEONARD CRIMSON

CONTENTS

CHAPTER 1

Introduction

When the OverVens first arrived in Denmark, they were taken aback by the high expectations for young children. For example, it was common for children to start learning the mandolin at an early age, while other activities, like bike riding, seemed to be less encouraged. Additionally, mothers in their neighborhood had a practice of leaving babies outside to nap, regardless of the weather. Despite her initial surprise, Christine OverVen found several Danish practices she admired and decided to adopt them.

One notable practice was the Danish approach to handling tantrums. Christine noticed that Danish parents did not reprimand their tantruming children, understanding that such reprimands often reinforced the negative behavior. This approach resonated with Christine, especially because her son, Laurits, who has Asperger's—a mild subtype of autism—required a sensitive and effective strategy to adjust to his new school environment. Christine's research into Danish child-rearing practices revealed that children raised in Denmark were generally more contented and adaptable in various situations.

In North America, there is a tendency to be judgmental about other countries, particularly regarding their parenting practices. Christine OverVen, a professor of communications studies at Longwood University in Virginia and an American expat raising her child in Denmark, experienced this judgment firsthand. Christine and her husband, both scientists, moved to Denmark in 2008 from Minneapolis with their then five-year-old son, Laurits. They had originally planned to stay for a year while Christiaan conducted post-doctoral research at the University of Copenhagen. However, they found the experience so enriching that they extended their stay twice.

Christine observed a clear difference in attitudes toward education and child-rearing between Denmark and the United States. While visiting the United States, she noticed that family gatherings often included judgmental comments based on misconceptions about Danish educational practices. Many people in the U.S. were curious about the age at which children in Denmark start kindergarten and made critical comments based on inaccurate information. Living in Copenhagen, Christine saw firsthand that Danish education and child-rearing practices were often misunderstood by outsiders.

In addition to the plethora of parenting advice available online and in print, Christine identified a troubling pattern of criticism toward different parenting styles. This tendency to judge other parents' choices, she believed, was counterproductive and often based on misinformation.

Cultural Influences on Parenting

Cultural influences play a significant role in shaping parenting practices. Different cultures have varying norms, values, and expectations that impact how parents raise their children. Let's dive deeper into these influences.

Italian Parenting Practices

When an Italian mother faced her daughter's refusal to drink milk, she sought advice from another adult. Instead of focusing on the behavior, the response emphasized the child's perceived bad nature: "Drink it, but drink it! Who can trust you? When will you ever learn about the good things I say? You're driven to destroy everything." This approach highlights a cultural tendency to address the child's character rather than specific actions, using past behavior to contextualize current issues. Such interactions reflect how Italian parents may prioritize socialization goals by emphasizing lessons learned from past events and making moral evaluations of the child's nature.

Hmong Parenting Practices

Similarly, a Hmong mother expressed her cultural parenting goals by telling her daughter, "That makes you a very bad girl," translating to "message what Bak" in Spanish. This phrase, meaning "It takes out," suggests that the child is inherently bad and must recognize and change her behavior. The emphasis on the child's responsibility to correct her actions indicates a temporary state of 'losing oneself' when behaving badly, reflecting the socialization process in Hmong culture.

Emotional Expressiveness and Physical Warmth

Emotional expressiveness and physical warmth are aspects of parenting that vary significantly across cultures. Interviews with mothers from different cultural backgrounds reveal that while the overall goals of parenting might be similar, the methods and emphasis on these elements differ. Some cultures value direct emotional expression and physical affection, while others may prioritize restraint and emotional control.

Traditional Practices

In traditional societies, such as the Amazonian foragers or the Quichean Mayas of Guatemala, children experience a childhood with few rules and limits. Anthropologist Richard P. Hewes noted that foragers largely allowed children the same freedoms as adults, mirroring the philosophies of European thinkers like John Locke and Rousseau. In these societies, children are integrated into the adult world through an apprenticeship of life, guided by their interests. These societies, characterized by decentralized and classless structures, expose children to less violence compared to those in more complex societies.

With the advent of modern conveniences and globalization, child-rearing practices have diversified. In Brazilian hunter-gatherer societies like the Suya, for instance, mothers and baby-carrying siblings adapt their movements to accommodate nursing standing up, distributing the baby's weight across their shoulders or back. Beyond infancy, child-rearing becomes a collective effort, with older siblings, aunts, and grandmothers sharing parenting duties.

Role of Religion

Religious practices significantly influence parenting. Research has linked religious adherence to parental forgiveness and future expectations for children. Religious scholars consider religion a crucial variable in predicting immigrant parents' child-rearing practices in the United States and other countries. While this study does not aim to evaluate the superiority of religious over non-religious parenting, it explores the impact of religious practices on child-rearing.

Religious beliefs shape the values and skills deemed essential for children and dictate the practices believed to foster spiritual development. Despite differences among world religions, they share a concern for timeless virtues and methods to achieve them. Religions reflect their originating cultures, with higher religiosity often found in collectivist societies that emphasize community harmony. As such, understanding the independent role of religion in parenting is vital. Major world religions—Islam, Judaism, Christianity, Hinduism, and Native American religions—provide clear symbols of faith, places of worship, and written rules that guide parenting practices.

Impact of Social Norms

Parenting behaviors are influenced by the values, ideas, and social norms of a society. Understanding the interplay of individual and cultural factors is crucial for effective parenting strategies. Research into the similarities and differences of child-rearing practices across cultures can enhance the core concepts of parenting, promoting children's safety, health, cognitive development, self-esteem, social competence, and independence.

In Japan, child socialization is aimed at grooming children to harmonize with society by supporting and helping one another. This process, rooted in atarimae (basic common sense), maintains social order through communication, cultural inheritance, and societal roles. However, as families adopt varying child-rearing methods, the weakening of this common sense poses challenges. To ensure the transmission of these values to future generations, it is essential to uphold the principles of Match-Borrow-Lend and respect traditional child-rearing concepts.

CHAPTER 3

Parenting Styles Across Countries

Parenting is the initial source of affection, possibilities, and control, providing protection against harmful forces in various cultural contexts. Research on parenting styles, particularly within different cultural settings, highlights global concerns regarding dimensions such as warmth, obedience, self-assuredness, and positive behavioral outcomes.

Studies indicate that cultural values and concerns significantly shape parenting styles, with each region prioritizing different psychological norms essential for children's success. A comprehensive literature review compares parenting styles in diverse countries, including the United States of America (USA), Armenia, Canada, China, Italy, Norway, Thailand, and Turkey, focusing on global differences in parenting dimensions, discipline, warmth, behavioral control, and parental expectations.

Over the last five decades, research has highlighted the diversity of parenting styles, revealing how they vary from one culture to another. Early research aimed to identify how parenting impacts adolescent development, but subsequent studies have further illustrated the cultural context of parenting practices.

Authoritarian Parenting

Several international meta-analytic studies, which aggregate data from numerous studies to assess averages and trends, find small to moderate associations between general measures of authoritarian parenting and children's externalizing behaviors, typically defined as aggressive or unadjusted behavior. These associations hold true across various cultural groups, including immigrant families, indicating the consistency of these findings.

Authoritarian parenting, the most well-researched type globally, relies on controlling strategies and confrontational discipline methods. This approach is based on the belief that such methods are necessary for children's development and effectiveness in achieving desired goals. Authoritarian parents often hold negative views of children, believing they are naturally unruly and must be strictly controlled without excessive praise.

Permissive Parenting

Permissive parenting, often associated with indulgent qualities, varies significantly across cultures. In the United States, permissive parenting is linked to high self-esteem, less delinquent behavior, and reasonable academic performance. However, this style is perceived differently in other cultures, such as China, where US parenting is seen as overly permissive. Cultural differences in parenting forums highlight how parents in different regions perceive and discuss their child-rearing practices.

Authoritative Parenting

Authoritative parenting, combining control with warmth and guidance, is prevalent in various cultures. In the United States, this approach involves treating children as independent individuals from an early age. In contrast, Asian parents, including Chinese and Chinese-American families, adopt a more controlling yet nurturing approach. They guide their children closely, emphasizing practice and improvement in skills such as piano, math, and kindness, while maintaining warmth and affection.

Uninvolved Parenting

Uninvolved parenting, characterized by low demands and low responsiveness, transcends national boundaries. Children of uninvolved parents often exhibit low levels of social interaction and prosocial behavior. This parenting style is associated with poverty and social policy issues, as seen in various low-income contexts worldwide. Uninvolved parents make minimal attempts to control their children, show little involvement in their lives, and have low expectations for self-control and self-regulation.

CHAPTER 4

Parent-Child Relationships

Gerard Jones has been a widely read columnist and author of parenting books, recognized in the media and the psychological community. Despite the various challenges in parenting, the importance of what parents communicate to their children remains a universal concern that transcends cultural differences. Attachment parenting, a concept emphasizing emotional bonding, is one of the fundamental elements of childrearing across societies. This close emotional connection not only provides psychological security for children during their early years but also continues to influence their adult lives.

Attachment Theory

Attachment theory posits that a secure emotional bond between parent and child is crucial for the child's psychological and emotional development. The theory suggests that the quality of attachment, measured through various means, is a vital indicator of a child's psychological security and is central to early childrearing practices. Across cultures, attachment parenting is seen as an emotional undertaking, with parents striving to create a nurturing and secure environment for their children.

In Europe and the UK, discussions about parenting often challenge stereotypes and highlight the importance of flexibility and open-mindedness in child-rearing practices. For example, the stereotype of the infallible Italian mother who excels in all aspects of childcare is criticized for being unrealistic and potentially harmful. Instead, there is an emphasis on addressing the underlying issues of anxiety, depression, and resentment that can affect parenting.

A comprehensive examination of attachment theory and parenting styles across cultures reveals significant concerns about pushing preschool children to achieve academic success at the expense of their emotional and developmental needs. International perspectives highlight the importance of addressing these issues with a balanced approach, considering the benefits of multi-language use and the impacts of early experiences on children's cognitive and emotional development.

Parental Bonding

Parental bonding is a cornerstone of family relationships, with research showing that parental warmth is a universal aspect of childrearing, though its expression may vary across cultures. Studies emphasize that early childhood bonding is crucial for children's overall development. For example, in Western cultures, authoritative parenting, characterized by warmth and structured guidance, has been shown to promote positive behaviors and attitudes in children. However, this does not mean that a strict set of principles is universally applicable; cultural variations must be considered to establish effective parenting programs.

Comparative studies, such as those by Kawamura, have examined self-esteem in children from different cultures. Findings indicate that American children generally have higher self-esteem compared to Japanese children, possibly due to more direct exposure to rewards and praise. However, the impact of a mother's verbal suggestions on a child's self-esteem highlights the complexity of parental influence, suggesting that positive reinforcement alone may not be sufficient to foster healthy self-esteem.

Parental Involvement

Parental involvement in a child's education and development is a critical factor in their success. Studies have shown that parents' expectations and involvement in their children's education vary significantly across cultures. For example, parents in the United States tend to spend less time helping with their children's education and have lower expectations for academic achievement compared to parents in Taiwan. This discrepancy underscores the importance of cultural context in understanding parental involvement.

Parental involvement encompasses various activities, including supervising school activities, meeting with teachers, and participating in parent-teacher meetings (PTMs). The level of involvement can influence a child's academic performance and overall development. Studies suggest that active parental involvement in both school and home settings contributes to better educational outcomes and socialization.

Research also indicates that differences in parental expectations and children's academic achievements are influenced by cultural norms and values. For example, parents in Japan and France are more likely to assist with homework and have higher academic expectations for their children compared to parents in the United States. Understanding these cultural differences is essential for developing effective parenting strategies that support children's development.

CHAPTER 5

Education and Discipline

Education and discipline practices vary widely across cultures, reflecting deep-seated values and societal norms. This chapter delves into the contrasting approaches and philosophies surrounding these aspects of child-rearing.

Approaches to Education

In European-American families, children are often encouraged to express their opinions, and adults are expected to listen, even if the child's views are not fully developed. This contrasts sharply with Italian families, where children are taught that commenting on the behavior and choices of others is impolite. Italian parents often view those who let themselves be "manipulated" by children as lacking proper education.

In Asian cultures, such as among the Singaporean Chinese, obedience and respect for authority are paramount. This cultural emphasis makes it easier for adults to socialize, educate, and discipline children consistently. In a Western-European family, a child is encouraged to express opinions, whereas, in a Chinese context, children are expected to obey without contradiction and to maintain good manners in all situations.

The Japanese education system is highly pressurizing, leaving little time for leisure and cultural activities. In contrast, several European countries provide more support to families, allowing for greater involvement from extended family members and social services designed to balance work and family life effectively.

Comparison studies indicate that cultural differences in education strategies extend from infancy and are influenced by a variety of sources, including family, teachers, and societal norms. These differences highlight the importance of involving the entire household and community in the educational process, as seen in the best-performing Nordic countries.

Discipline Strategies

Discipline strategies are also culturally influenced. For example, in some cultures, practices such as throat singing in Mongolia and Russia or "crying it out" in Japan are accepted, while global media exposure has led to an increased acceptance of both authoritarian and permissive child-rearing styles in Western societies.

Parents' beliefs about acceptable behavior for children vary widely. In Japan, toddlers are expected to sit independently by 18 months, while American toddlers are often held by their parents for as long as possible. Korean children are raised in an environment that emphasizes group over self-interest and instills a sense of shame over guilt, encouraging obedience and care for parents.

The socialization of children through parental nurturing, rules, and discipline is closely tied to cultural values and expectations. These practices are influenced by the broader cultural and social contexts in which parents operate.

Importance of Academic Achievement

Cultural values also impact the emphasis placed on academic achievement and social participation. Collectivist cultures, such as those in parts of Asia and the Middle East, prioritize social coherence and interdependence. In contrast, Western cultures often emphasize individual self-discovery and independence.

Parents universally desire their children to succeed in school and life. However, the emphasis varies: collectivist cultures focus more on academic achievement, while individualistic cultures prioritize personal happiness and self-fulfillment. For example, parents in the United States tend to emphasize personal happiness and independence, whereas parents in Korea, Japan, Taiwan, and Turkey place a greater emphasis on academic success and social obligations.

CHAPTER 6

Parenting Challenges in a Globalized World

Globalization has introduced a wealth of cultural diversity into child-rearing practices, providing opportunities for parents to adopt and integrate complementary features from different traditions. However, this blending of cultures can also result in identity issues and confusion for parents navigating cross-cultural boundaries. The internet further complicates matters by offering an abundance of parenting advice with international dimensions.

Cultural Conflicts

First-generation immigrant families often face complex challenges as they navigate between their cultural heritage and the norms of their new environment. The Immigration and Refugee Board of Canada describes socialization as a process where children learn cultural practices, expectations, and values within a cultural context. Immigrant parents must balance the retention of their cultural identity with the need to adapt to new societal norms, creating a dynamic environment for their children's development.

Acculturation and acculturative stress are significant issues for immigrant families, impacting language choices, behavioral expectations, and adherence to traditional values. Understanding how these families manage cultural socialization at home is crucial to supporting their integration and success.

Balancing Tradition and Modernity

The collapse of the Soviet Union left Russian parents in a state of "in between," struggling to balance old traditions with modern practices. Trauma from the past and external pressures have hindered the transmission of family traditions, making the synthesis of old and new child-rearing practices a critical focus for Russian parents. This struggle is not unique to Russia but is seen in many societies worldwide.

For example, a Russian mother describing her child as "practical" reflects deep-rooted cultural values of independence, strength, and adherence to traditional norms. These values, stemming from historical and religious influences, emphasize obedience, honor, hard work, and respect for elders.

Impact of Technology

Technology plays a significant role in modern parenting, with different cultures adopting varied approaches. In Japan and Korea, the use of the internet in schools has prompted parents to develop technology usage rules. Russian parents may allow more water time in lessons for infants, reflecting cultural preferences and practices.

Privacy concerns and the use of technology for monitoring children vary across cultures. For instance, American parents may be reluctant to use tracking cell phones, while over 90% of Japanese children have them for emergency purposes. The use of technology, such as robot animals and iPods, also reflects cultural adaptations to modern challenges.

Surprisingly, despite the centrality of technology in children's lives, there is limited literature on its impact. This area remains a Western concern, with many parents in other countries taking a more casual approach. Understanding these cultural differences is essential for developing effective strategies to address the challenges of technology in parenting.

CHAPTER 7

Parenting and Child Development

This chapter explores how cultural practices reflect the embeddedness of infants within their social worlds and emphasizes the importance of considering parent-infant dyads within the broader web of family relationships. Cultural perspectives on parent-child relationships can enhance or constrain individuation and autonomy, key interests of developmental and social psychologists.

Cognitive Development

Cognitive development encompasses the mental processes involved in perceiving, learning, thinking, and understanding. In India, education involves learning multiple scripts and languages within constrained infrastructures, particularly in rural areas. The unequal spread of computer access and high birth rates further influence self-regulation skills and cognitive development.

Modern biology, medicine, and technology have greatly influenced our understanding of child development, making present generations highly skilled digital users. Empirical evidence highlights unique cultural influences on cognitive functioning worldwide, challenging accepted developmental theories primarily derived from Western societies.

Emotional Development

Emotional development involves the child's ability to express and manage emotions. Cultural practices, such as the specific vocalizations used by Fulani children in Nigeria, illustrate how laughter and interaction serve as bond-strengthening agents. Joint research by Canadians, Swedes, and the Fulani demonstrates varied communication patterns between parents and infants, highlighting cultural differences in emotional development.

Studies show that early interactions, such as parental responses to infant vocalizations, play a crucial role in emotional bonding and development. These interactions vary across cultures, reflecting the diverse ways parents nurture their children's emotional growth.

Social Development

Social development begins at birth, with infants seeking eye contact and responding to their mother's voice. Cultural differences in parenting strategies influence how social skills and behaviors are nurtured. In collectivistic cultures like China, parents emphasize social trust and reinforce behaviors that promote social coherence. In contrast, individualistic cultures prioritize personal achievement and self-reliance.

Research suggests that the roots of social cognition are deep-seated, with early experiments showing differences in how infants from various cultures engage in social activities. Understanding these cultural variations is essential for appreciating the diverse pathways to social development.

CHAPTER 8

Parenting Support and Resources

Parenting support and resources are essential for providing guidance and assistance to parents, helping them navigate the challenges of child-rearing. The widespread availability of these resources indicates a strong belief in their potential to improve family life.

Government Programs

Government programs play a significant role in providing parenting support. In Sweden, for example, the government offers a robust parental advisory service (BVC), which is widely used by parents. Sweden's family policies, such as paid parental leave, reflect internationally recognized child-rearing values and promote a supportive environment for parents. These programs aim to enhance the early parent-child relationship and prevent issues such as child abuse, contributing to national development and stability.

Non-Profit Organizations

Non-profit organizations are crucial in disseminating research data and providing educational services. Organizations like the Minnesota MFT Association and the Society for Research in Child Development offer resources for family therapists and professionals, helping them enhance their cultural competence. These organizations facilitate the exchange of knowledge and best practices, supporting diverse client populations. Non-profits also conduct research and provide forums for discussions on child development, mental health, and cultural diversity.

Online Communities

Online communities provide valuable support for expatriate, refugee, and migrant families. These communities offer a platform for sharing personal stories, strategies, and resources, helping parents navigate unique challenges. Blogs, discussion boards, and social media groups enable parents to connect with others in similar situations, fostering a sense of community and support. For example, adoptive parents from Korea can access online resources and information to help them through the adoption process.

CHAPTER 9

Parenting Practices and Mental Health

Parenting practices significantly influence the mental health of children and adolescents. High levels of sensitivity to a child's emotional needs, combined with moderately demanding behavioral expectations, are regarded as the most effective guidelines for ethical child-rearing. These core competencies are essential for promoting children's personal competencies, leading to improved economic opportunities and quality of life.

Parental Stress

Parental stress can vary significantly depending on cultural context and societal norms. In a comprehensive 34-country study involving 36,022 two-year-old children, it was found that certain variables consistently predicted higher levels of parental stress. These included children's behavior problems, parental depressive symptoms, marital stressors, family violence, and parental work interruptions. These factors collectively contribute to high levels of child-driven parental stress, which can be exacerbated by the fast pace of societal changes such as technology advancements, economic shifts, and evolving employment landscapes.

For example, parents who are accustomed to the rapid changes in children's social, psychological, and healthcare environments may experience heightened anxiety and stress about effectively nurturing their child's development. This stress is further compounded by a potential decline in belief or commitment to the traditional 'duty' of parenting. The modern economic environment, with its demands for dual-income households and less time available for parenting, also adds to the stress levels of parents.

Postpartum Depression (PPD)

Postpartum depression (PPD) manifests differently across various cultural contexts, influenced by societal norms, religious practices, and traditional beliefs. PPD is characterized by severe emotional distress following childbirth and can significantly impact a mother's ability to care for her newborn. In many Western societies, PPD is well-documented and treated through medical and psychological interventions. However, in non-Western cultures, the understanding and expression of PPD can be quite different.

For instance, in some traditional societies, there may not be a specific term for depression, but equivalents exist in the form of emotional or somatic complaints. In some African cultures, PPD might manifest as marked impoverishment or, in severe cases, infanticide or post-natal suicide. In Asian cultures, PPD may be expressed through social withdrawal or avoidance following childbirth, accompanied by physical symptoms such as unexplained chest pain or panic-like symptoms.

A culturally-relative approach to understanding PPD involves considering the unique societal "lenses" that shape experiences and responses to the condition. The HERITAGE model, which examines Health, Economics, Relationships, Infant care, Tradition, Age, Governance, and Emotion, provides a framework for understanding how these factors interplay to influence PPD in different societies.

This model highlights the importance of considering cultural context when diagnosing and treating PPD to ensure effective and culturally sensitive interventions.

Impact on Child's Mental Health

Parenting practices directly impact the mental health of children and adolescents. Research indicates that children who do not engage in extended play with their parents are at higher risk of developing emotional and behavioral health issues. The quality and quantity of parent-supervised playtime can significantly influence a child's mental health, promoting positive behaviors and reducing the risk of hyperactivity and conduct problems.

For example, a study involving Greek adolescents found that authoritative parenting practices, which combine warmth and structure, are protective factors for mental health. Children who experience consistent parental supervision during their free time are less likely to exhibit emotional and behavioral problems. This finding underscores the importance of supportive and structured parenting in fostering positive mental health outcomes.

Additionally, cross-cultural studies have shown that parenting practices can vary widely in their impact on children's mental health. In collectivistic cultures, where social trust and community coherence are emphasized, children are often socialized to prioritize group harmony and obedience. This socialization process can contribute to a sense of stability and security, which is beneficial for mental health. In contrast, individualistic cultures may place a greater emphasis on personal achievement and independence, which can foster self-reliance and self-esteem but may also lead to increased pressure and stress.

Understanding these cultural variations is crucial for developing effective parenting strategies that support children's mental health. By considering the unique cultural contexts and adapting parenting practices accordingly, parents can provide a nurturing environment that promotes the well-being of their children.

CHAPTER 10

Parenting in Different Socioeconomic Contexts

The socioeconomic context in which parents raise their children significantly affects parenting practices and the resources available for child-rearing. This chapter explores how these contexts create varying opportunities and challenges for parents, highlighting the differences between countries like the United States, Sweden, and others.

Poverty and Parenting

Low- and middle-income countries together represent 85% of the world's population. In these regions, economic challenges and political pressures erode the rights and resources critical for family security. Even as some middle-income countries continue to grow economically, they still host the majority of global poverty. The daily lives of families in impoverished communities are shaped by a lack of resources, leading to heightened family stress and vulnerability.

In low- and middle-income countries, mothers often focus on ensuring their children's basic needs are met, such as health, safety, and nurturance. However, the scarcity of resources makes it difficult to address these concerns adequately. The stress from deprivation compounds family vulnerability, making it challenging for parents to provide the necessary support for their children's development.

For example, in many parts of sub-Saharan Africa and South Asia, families face significant barriers to accessing quality healthcare, education, and nutrition. These challenges are often exacerbated by unstable political environments and economic policies that do not prioritize the well-being of the poorest populations. Consequently, parents in these regions must navigate a complex web of obstacles to support their children's growth and development.

Affluence and Parenting

Affluent parenting, on the other hand, is associated with greater access to resources and opportunities. Children from wealthy families often receive longer and better education and have better job prospects later in life. However, the benefits of affluence are not without challenges. Consumption habits among affluent youth, such as substance misuse and unhealthy eating, are areas of concern that have often been addressed with moralistic and punitive solutions rather than constructive engagement.

Quinlivan and Swan's research on affluent parenting in Australia reveals that households with children spent significant amounts on entertainment, audio-visual equipment, and dining out. While these expenditures reflect a high standard of living, they also highlight the consumer-driven nature of modern parenting. The focus on material goods and experiences can sometimes overshadow the importance of fostering meaningful connections and cultural enrichment.

In affluent societies, parents may also face pressures to ensure their children achieve high levels of success. This can lead to a highly competitive environment where children are pushed to excel academically and in extracurricular activities. While this drive for success can result in positive outcomes, it can also lead to increased stress and anxiety for both parents and children.

Intergenerational Transmission of Education

The intergenerational transmission of education is another aspect influenced by socioeconomic context. In the United States, higher income levels are closely tied to human capital, with wealthier families often able to invest more in their children's education. In contrast, Sweden places a stronger emphasis on education transmission through schools, making educational opportunities more equitable across different income levels.

Braun and Krighammer's comparison of the United States and Sweden highlights how these differing approaches impact children's educational attainment. In Sweden, the return on education is increasing, leading to a more pronounced intergenerational transmission of education. This suggests that the country's education system is effectively reducing the influence of socioeconomic disparities on children's educational outcomes. In the United States, however, the decreasing return on education and the strong link between income and education contribute to greater disparities in educational attainment.

The Cost of Parenting

The cost of parenting varies significantly across different socioeconomic contexts. Parents in wealthier societies may have the means to pay for high-quality childcare, extracurricular activities, and private education. Conversely, parents in poorer regions may struggle to afford basic necessities, let alone additional resources for their children's development.

Understanding the economic perspective on parenting costs provides insight into the varying challenges faced by parents. For instance, parents in affluent societies might pay substantial amounts for professional childcare services, while those in low-income regions rely on extended family and community support. These differences highlight the diverse strategies parents use to navigate the economic realities of their respective contexts.

CHAPTER 11

Gender Roles and Parenting

Gender roles significantly influence parenting practices across different cultures. The expectations and responsibilities assigned to mothers and fathers can shape how children are raised and impact their development. This chapter explores traditional and changing gender roles in parenting and how these roles vary across countries.

Traditional Gender Roles

Traditionally, gender roles have dictated specific responsibilities for mothers and fathers. In many cultures, mothers are primarily responsible for childcare and household duties, while fathers are seen as the breadwinners. These roles, however, are evolving in various parts of the world.

In Japan, women's participation in society decreases significantly after having children. Mothers often find themselves solely responsible for childcare, while fathers work long hours. This traditional division of labor can be challenging for women who wish to balance work and family life. In contrast, Denmark has seen a shift towards more involved fatherhood. Danish fathers are increasingly sharing tasks such as cooking, bathing, and playing with their children, especially on weekends.

In many European countries, such as France and Sweden, men are also more involved in childcare. These countries encourage shared parenting responsibilities, with fathers actively participating in child-rearing activities. However, this is less common in some other cultures where traditional gender roles remain deeply ingrained.

For instance, in India, the father's role is often seen as the primary educator and disciplinarian, while the mother takes on the nurturing and caregiving responsibilities. This division is still evident in many households, although some families are beginning to embrace more egalitarian practices.

Changing Gender Roles

Compared to previous generations, today's young adults are more open-minded about the roles of men and women in the family. This shift is particularly noticeable among men, who are increasingly adopting more egalitarian attitudes towards gender roles. Family background plays a significant role in shaping these attitudes, with individuals often inheriting their views from their parents.

Social and demographic changes are driving a global movement towards gender equality, aiming to give boys and girls equal opportunities from an early age. International institutions like the United Nations and global NGOs are actively promoting gender equity as a fundamental human right and a key factor in achieving sustainable development.

In many parts of the world, efforts to challenge and redefine traditional gender roles are gaining momentum. For example, in Israel, it is common for parents to share childcare duties and work relatively equal hours. This approach not only benefits the children but also promotes a healthier work-life balance for both parents.

Similarly, in the United States, the "Lean In" campaign and other initiatives are advocating for workplace policies that better accommodate mothers. This includes on-ramps and off-ramps, sabbaticals, mentoring, and bias-free hiring practices. Despite these efforts, the U.S. still lags behind many Western, industrialized countries in terms of family leave policies and economic opportunities for women.

Gender and Parenting Practices

Gender roles also influence specific parenting practices, such as how parents feed their babies, teach them to sleep, and understand developmental milestones. In France, for example, parents often emphasize the importance of teaching children to sleep through the night from an early age. In contrast, Japanese parents may have different expectations for baby milestones and child-rearing practices.

Understanding these cultural variations in gender roles and parenting practices is crucial for recognizing the diverse ways in which families navigate the challenges of raising children. By acknowledging and addressing these differences, societies can work towards more inclusive and supportive environments for all parents, regardless of gender.

CHAPTER 12

Parenting in Multicultural Families

The dynamics of multicultural families present unique challenges and opportunities for parenting. This chapter explores the experiences of children and parents in multicultural families and examines the implications for pedagogical practices and multicultural policies.

Blended Families

Blended families, where one or both partners have children from previous relationships, have become increasingly common in Western societies. These family structures challenge traditional notions of parenthood that are closely tied to biological relationships. From a sociological perspective, being a parent is a societal construct rather than a purely biological one. This understanding is crucial for recognizing the diverse forms of parenthood that exist today.

In blended families, stepparenting is a significant aspect. Stepparents often take on parental responsibilities for their partner's children, creating complex family dynamics. Research in this area focuses on the impact of a biology-only view of parenthood on our understanding of step-mothering and other non-biological parental roles. Recognizing the importance of these roles is essential for supporting children and parents in blended families.

Intercultural Marriages

Intercultural marriages, where partners come from different cultural backgrounds, present unique challenges in parenting. These couples often navigate diverse child-rearing practices and must find a balance that works for their family. The process of negotiating child-rearing strategies in intercultural marriages can be enriching, prompting interest in learning about different languages, foods, and cultural practices.

Social scientists have studied how international couples achieve balanced child-rearing strategies. The solutions are varied and depend on factors such as the targeted outcomes for their children, each parent's time availability, national regulations, and social support networks. Through interviews and daily interactions, these couples develop strategies that incorporate the best aspects of both cultures.

The increasing frequency of intermarriages highlights the importance of open communication and negotiation in parenting. Couples must discuss and reconcile their differing child-rearing practices to ensure a harmonious family life. This process involves not only the parents but also extended family members and social networks, contributing to a richer and more diverse parenting experience.

Multicultural Challenges and Opportunities

Multicultural families often face unique challenges, such as navigating different cultural expectations and dealing with potential conflicts between cultural norms. However, these challenges also present opportunities for growth and learning. Children in multicultural families are exposed to diverse perspectives and experiences, which can foster greater cultural awareness and adaptability.

Parenting in multicultural families requires flexibility and openness to different approaches. Parents must be willing to adapt their practices to accommodate multiple cultural influences. This flexibility can lead to innovative parenting strategies that blend the strengths of each culture, providing a richer environment for children's development.

Policy and Practice Implications

The experiences of multicultural families have important implications for policy and practice. Educators, social workers, and policymakers need to consider the diverse needs of multicultural families when developing programs and services. This includes creating inclusive environments that respect and celebrate cultural diversity.

Policies should also support the unique needs of multicultural families, such as language support for non-native speakers and cultural competency training for service providers. By addressing these needs, society can help ensure that multicultural families receive the support they need to thrive.

CHAPTER 13

Parenting and Technology

The integration of technology into parenting has transformed the ways in which families interact, learn, and communicate. This chapter explores the intersections between traditional practices and modern technology, the concept of digital parenting, and strategies for managing screen time.

Digital Parenting

Digital parenting refers to the practices parents adopt to manage their children's use of digital technology. The concept of digital immigrants highlights the generational gap between those who grew up without digital technology and those who are digital natives. This gap can influence how children learn and interact with technology, as well as how parents guide and monitor their digital experiences.

The advent of digital technology has opened up numerous learning opportunities that previous generations did not have. However, this technological experience can also change the way children learn, raising questions about the relevance of traditional teaching methods. Digital parenting does not follow a standardized approach but rather involves a flexible and adaptive process where parents navigate the digital environment to ensure positive educational outcomes for their children.

Digital parenting practices include setting limits on screen time, monitoring online activities, and ensuring that the digital content children consume is age-appropriate and educational. It also involves guiding children on how to use technology responsibly and safely. While technology can be a valuable tool for learning, it is essential for parents to balance digital and non-digital activities to support their children's overall development.

Screen Time Management

Managing screen time is a critical aspect of digital parenting. Children today have access to a wide range of digital devices and platforms, from smartphones to tablets and smart speakers. While these devices can offer educational benefits, excessive screen time can lead to various problems, including attention issues, sleep disturbances, and obesity.

The American Academy of Pediatrics (AAP) provides guidelines for managing screen time based on the age of the child. For infants and toddlers (under 18 months), screen time should be avoided, except for video chatting. For children aged 18 to 24 months, high-quality programming can be introduced with adult co-viewing to ensure the child is engaging in interactive and meaningful activities.

For preschool-aged children (2 to 5 years), the AAP recommends limiting screen time to one hour per day of high-quality programming. Parents should co-view media with their children to help them understand what they are seeing and apply it to the world around them. For school-aged children and teens, the focus should be on balancing screen time with other activities, including physical exercise, sleep, and face-to-face interactions.

Benefits and Challenges of Technology

Technology offers several benefits for children's learning and development. Educational apps, online resources, and interactive games can enhance cognitive skills, improve language abilities, and provide opportunities for creative expression. However, the challenges associated with technology use cannot be overlooked.

One of the primary concerns is the potential for digital addiction, where children become overly dependent on digital devices for entertainment and social interaction. This dependency can impact their physical health, social skills, and academic performance. Parents need to be vigilant and proactive in setting boundaries and encouraging a healthy balance between digital and non-digital activities.

Additionally, the internet can expose children to inappropriate content and online risks such as cyberbullying, privacy breaches, and predatory behaviors. Digital parenting involves educating children about online safety, monitoring their online activities, and using parental control tools to block harmful content.

Cultural Perspectives on Digital Parenting

Cultural differences also play a role in digital parenting practices. For example, some cultures may emphasize strict limits on screen time and prioritize face-to-face interactions, while others may be more lenient with digital use as part of their daily routines. Understanding these cultural perspectives can help parents adopt practices that align with their values and support their children's development.

In her study, sociolinguist Ilana Shison-Cennamo explores how low-income, single immigrant mothers from diverse cultural backgrounds navigate digital parenting. These mothers face unique challenges related to migration, poverty, literacy, and access to technology. By raising awareness of these challenges, Shison-Cennamo aims to ensure that children from these backgrounds can benefit from educational opportunities, such as Gifted and Talented programs.

CHAPTER 14

Parenting and Health

Parenting practices play a crucial role in the health and well-being of children. This chapter explores how parenting influences nutrition, physical health, sleep, rest, hygiene, and safety, providing insights into the diverse approaches taken by different cultures.

Nutrition and Physical Health

Childhood nutrition and health are fundamental to the development of a child's immune system and overall well-being. Parents can guide the development of their children's immune systems by being aware of the sources of bacteria and viruses that colonize their bodies. Factors such as improvements in sanitation, access to appropriate antibiotics, antiviral medications, and proper breastfeeding habits play a significant role in shaping health outcomes.

The human microbiome, the collection of microorganisms residing in and on our bodies, is crucial for maintaining health. These microorganisms can be commensal (sharing our bodies without interaction) or symbiotic (benefiting from the host relationship). For example, gut bacteria help break down complex carbohydrates and establish our immune defenses. Maintaining a delicate balance between these microorganisms and our immune cells is essential for health, and disruptions can have immediate and long-term consequences.

Parents can make informed decisions about their children's diet, physical activities, and healthcare by understanding the factors that influence health outcomes. For instance, exposure to diverse environments and natural elements can strengthen the immune system, while balanced nutrition supports overall physical health.

Sleep and Rest

Sleep is a critical component of children's health, influencing their cognitive development, emotional well-being, and physical growth. Cultural attitudes towards sleep vary significantly, impacting how parents approach bedtime routines and sleep training.

In the United States, there is a strong emphasis on independence and self-sufficiency, leading to practices such as sleep training. American parents often endure sleepless nights as they teach their children to soothe themselves to sleep, a process rooted in the belief that self-soothing is an essential social lesson. However, this approach can be exhausting for parents and may not always align with global norms.

In contrast, other cultures may prioritize co-sleeping or more relaxed bedtime routines, focusing on nurturing close parent-child bonds. These practices reflect different cultural values and beliefs about the importance of independence versus interconnectedness.

Hygiene and Safety

Hygiene and safety are paramount concerns for parents across cultures, though the specific practices and beliefs can vary widely. For example, in the United Arab Emirates, traditional beliefs and practices influence how parents care for their children's health and safety. Some Emirati parents adhere to old wives' tales, such as not changing a baby's clothes during overcast days to avoid illness or using amulets (taweez) featuring Qur'anic verses to ward off sickness.

While some of these practices may seem superstitious, they reflect a deep-seated concern for children's well-being. Similarly, parents in the United States may have their own sets of worries and precautions, such as preventing sudden infant death syndrome (SIDS) and ensuring overall safety.

Understanding and respecting these cultural differences in hygiene and safety practices can provide valuable insights into how parents navigate the challenges of protecting their children. By combining traditional wisdom with modern healthcare practices, parents can create a balanced approach to ensuring their children's health and safety.

Health Infrastructure and Cultural Practices

The health outcomes of children are also influenced by the broader health infrastructure and cultural practices in their societies. For instance, access to quality healthcare, clean water, and nutritious food can significantly impact children's health. In many low- and middle-income countries, these resources may be limited, leading to higher rates of infectious diseases and malnutrition.

Cultural practices, such as breastfeeding and traditional remedies, also play a role in shaping health outcomes. While some traditional practices are beneficial, others may need to be adapted or supplemented with modern healthcare interventions to ensure the best outcomes for children.

CHAPTER 15

Parenting and Discipline Strategies

Discipline strategies are a fundamental aspect of parenting, influencing the development and behavior of children. This chapter explores various discipline approaches, including positive discipline, time-outs, and consequences, with a focus on how these strategies are implemented in different cultural contexts.

Positive Discipline

Positive discipline emphasizes a balanced approach between meeting children's needs and setting limits and expectations. It focuses on teaching and guiding children rather than punishing them. The goal is to help children develop self-discipline, responsibility, and problem-solving skills.

Positive discipline involves several key strategies:

- **Clear Communication**: Parents talk with their children and clearly explain what behavior is expected and why certain actions are inappropriate.
- **Rule Charts**: Creating charts with rules and consequences or rewards can help children understand what is expected of

them. Collaborating with children to set goals and celebrate achievements reinforces positive behavior.

- **Coaching**: When a child misbehaves, parents provide educational information and encourage the child to think of solutions. This approach helps children learn from their mistakes and develop critical thinking skills.
- **Emotional Awareness**: Parents recognize their own frustration and address it constructively, modeling emotional regulation for their children.

In many cultures, positive discipline is seen as an effective way to promote healthy development. For example, Bill 370/2006 on Positive Discipline in India emphasizes the importance of non-violent discipline methods and aims to reduce the use of corporal punishment. Studies support the effectiveness of positive discipline in reducing conflicts within families and improving relationships between parents and children.

Time-Outs and Consequences

Time-outs and consequences are commonly used discipline strategies, but their implementation and interpretation can vary widely across cultures.

Time-Outs: In the United States, time-outs are used to give children a break from a situation where they are misbehaving. The goal is to allow the child to calm down and reflect on their behavior. However, in Italy, the concept is similar but focuses more on reflection rather than punishment. Children are encouraged to think about what they have done and understand the impact of their actions.

Consequences: In Scandinavian countries, the concept of consequences is used to teach children the relationship between their actions and outcomes. Effort and good behavior are rewarded, while poor choices lead to natural consequences. This approach helps children understand that their actions have real-world implications and encourages them to make better decisions.

Spanking: Spanking, though controversial, is still used in some cultures as a disciplinary measure. In the United States, it is generally recommended only for young children (ages 2 to 4) and should be explained to the child beforehand. However, there is a growing movement against corporal punishment, with many experts advocating for non-violent discipline methods.

In the UK, psychoanalyst Margaret Rustin notes that traditional patterns of authority and discipline are evolving. Parents and teachers are increasingly using dialogue and explanations to guide children, reflecting a shift towards more interactive and intensive socialization methods.

Cultural Perspectives on Discipline

Discipline strategies are deeply influenced by cultural norms and values. For example, in India, traditional child-rearing practices are often authoritarian, with a strong emphasis on obedience and respect for authority. While this can lead to well-behaved children, it may also suppress creativity and independence.

In contrast, cultures that prioritize individualism, such as the United States, tend to encourage self-expression and autonomy. This can result in a more permissive approach to discipline, with a focus on fostering independence and critical thinking skills.

Understanding these cultural differences is crucial for developing effective discipline strategies that support children's development while respecting cultural values. By combining positive discipline with appropriate consequences, parents can create a balanced approach that promotes healthy behavior and emotional growth.

CHAPTER 16

Parenting and Social Media

The advent of the internet and technology has significantly impacted parenting practices across different cultural backgrounds. The internet provides access to a vast array of information, influences, and support networks, allowing parents to appreciate diverse child-rearing practices and move away from traditional methods. Social media, in particular, plays a crucial role in shaping modern parenting.

Sharing Parenting Experiences

One of the key aims of parenting is to ensure the survival and successful development of children into adulthood. In today's multicultural world, sharing different parenting experiences can bring great benefits. Intercultural families, in particular, can learn innovative and diverse ways of parenting as they naturally encounter varied methods in their daily lives.

Parents often look to others for advice and support, seeking guidance from family members, friends, teachers, and online communities. By collaborating with others and sharing their experiences, parents can feel more secure and confident in their parenting decisions. This exchange of knowledge helps parents navigate the challenges of raising children in a culturally diverse society.

Social media platforms provide a space for parents to connect, share experiences, and offer support to one another. Online communities and forums allow parents to discuss common challenges, seek advice, and share successes. This virtual support network can be especially valuable for parents who may not have access to a strong local support system.

Impact on Parent-Child Relationships

The balance between closeness and emotional distance in parent-child relationships is an important issue that varies across cultures. In North America, the concept of "quality time" is emphasized, though it may not have an equivalent term in other languages or cultures. This idea suggests that the amount of time spent with children is less important than the quality of interactions.

Affluent North American parents often receive parenting advice from various sources, including experts, bloggers, and media personalities. Navigating conflicting philosophies and finding effective practices can be challenging. Books like "Bringing Up Bébé" offer insights into different cultural approaches to parenting, providing an alternative perspective on child-rearing.

For instance, while American parents may rely on scientific advice and structured parenting methods, others may turn to family traditions or personal experiences. A Belgian college student described preferring advice from her mother or grandmother but relying on the internet for urgent questions. This illustrates how modern parents blend traditional knowledge with digital resources.

Influence of Social Media on Parenting

Social media has a profound impact on parenting practices. Parents use social media to share milestones, seek advice, and connect with other parents. These platforms provide a sense of community and support, allowing parents to share their joys and challenges in real-time.

However, social media can also create pressure to present an idealized version of parenting. The constant stream of curated images and success stories can lead to feelings of inadequacy and comparison. Parents may feel compelled to meet unrealistic standards, which can impact their self-esteem and mental health.

Despite these challenges, social media remains a valuable tool for parents. It offers access to a wealth of information, connects parents with similar experiences, and provides a platform for advocacy and support. By engaging with social media mindfully, parents can benefit from its positive aspects while mitigating its potential drawbacks.

Cultural Variations in Social Media Use

The way parents use social media varies across cultures. In some cultures, social media is a primary source of parenting advice and support, while in others, traditional family and community structures play a more significant role. Understanding these cultural variations can help parents make informed decisions about their use of social media and digital technology.

For example, in cultures with strong extended family networks, parents may rely more on in-person advice and support. In contrast, parents in more individualistic societies may turn to online communities for guidance. These differences highlight the need for a nuanced approach to digital parenting, taking into account cultural values and practices.

CHAPTER 17

Parenting and Education

Parents play a critical role in their children's education, and their involvement can vary greatly across different cultural contexts. This chapter explores how parents from various countries balance academic guidance with encouraging self-discovery, the impact of early childhood education, homeschooling, and the role of extracurricular activities.

Early Childhood Education

Early childhood education is fundamental for the cognitive and social development of children. In many Nordic countries, preschool education is highly valued and widely attended. For example, in Finland, 97% of 6-year-olds attend preschool, with significant participation from younger age groups as well. The Finnish preschool system integrates play-based learning with academic activities, fostering a holistic development approach.

Parents in Finland, like their counterparts in the U.S. and Norway, prioritize both psychosocial and early literacy skills. However, there is often a misalignment between parents' goals and early childhood education professionals' goals, with the latter focusing more on academic skills. This highlights the need for a balanced approach that combines academic orientations with emotional and social development.

In contrast, countries like Uganda and Italy have different levels of parental involvement in early childhood education. In Uganda, parents rarely monitor their children's school performance, while in Italy, parental involvement is often limited to participation in the Parent's Teachers Association. This variation underscores the diverse educational landscapes and the importance of context-specific approaches to early childhood education.

Homeschooling

Homeschooling is an educational option that allows parents to take primary responsibility for their children's education. It is practiced in at least 23 countries worldwide, though its acceptance and regulation vary. In some countries, such as the Netherlands and Germany, homeschooling is legal but highly regulated. In others, it may be illegal but practiced unofficially.

Homeschooling can lead to positive outcomes, such as higher standardized test scores, greater civic engagement, and high social class jobs. However, it also faces criticism and negative perceptions in some cultures. For example, in Greece and the Netherlands, there are concerns about the lack of agreed-upon measures of school success and the influence of religious beliefs on homeschooling practices.

In countries where political restrictions limit homeschooling, distance education through the internet offers an alternative pathway. This allows parents to customize their children's education while adhering to national education laws. The diverse attitudes towards homeschooling reflect broader cultural, religious, and political factors influencing education systems.

Extracurricular Activities

Extracurricular activities play a crucial role in children's development by fostering intellectual, social, and moral growth. In countries like Switzerland, there is an emphasis on low-key and inexpensive extracurricular activities. Swiss parents prioritize creating a lively curiosity in music and other interests without placing undue pressure on children to excel.

In contrast, American parents often focus on year-round, potentially expensive sports and extracurricular activities, partly driven by the pressures of university applications. This competitive approach can sometimes lead to emotional stress for children and parents alike.

Norwegian families living in the United States express concerns about the time that American schools take away from family life. They emphasize the importance of moral preparation and emotional support in children's development. This highlights the need for balance between structured activities and free time for family interactions.

In choosing extracurricular activities, parents should consider their children's interests and the potential benefits of various activities. Encouraging children to explore different interests and develop a well-rounded skill set can contribute to their overall growth and well-being.

CHAPTER 18

Parenting and Teenagers

Parenting teenagers presents unique challenges and opportunities as young people navigate the transition from childhood to adulthood. This chapter explores the complexities of adolescent development, including adolescent rebellion and peer influence, while providing insights into how different cultures approach these issues.

Adolescent Rebellion

Adolescence is a period characterized by ambivalence and contradiction. Teenagers often seek independence while simultaneously feeling a strong need to belong. This stage of life is marked by a desire to distance themselves from childhood behaviors and responsibilities while not yet being fully prepared for adult life.

Historically, adolescence has been recognized as a distinct stage of development. The ancient Greeks were among the first to identify this transitional phase, and over time, societies have developed various approaches to managing the challenges associated with adolescence. The early Church, for example, focused on re-educating the nobility during this period, while the eighteenth century saw the concept of "ideal" adolescence emerge, emphasizing discovery and active participation in social and cultural progress.

Adolescent rebellion is a common theme in the literature on youth behavior and family relationships. Conflict between teenagers and their parents is almost universal, driven by both biological and social developmental processes. Adolescents are prone to display behaviors that defy adult expectations and challenge parental authority. However, the nature of these conflicts and the strategies for managing them vary widely across cultures.

In many cultures, attitudes toward adolescent conflict, methods of dealing with it, and the interpretation of its meaning are deeply rooted in cultural norms. For example, some societies may view adolescent rebellion as a normal and necessary part of growing up, while others may see it as a behavior that needs to be strictly controlled. Understanding these cultural differences is crucial for developing effective parenting strategies that support teenagers' development while maintaining healthy family relationships.

Peer Influence

Peer influence is a natural and significant aspect of adolescent development. It is one of the ways young people learn to become independent and form their own identities. The ability to be influenced by peers begins in early childhood and increases over time, often surpassing parental influence during adolescence.

In collectivistic cultures, such as those in Singapore and Malaysia, peer influence can be particularly intense due to the emphasis on group harmony and larger family households. Research suggests that adolescents in these cultures may experience stronger peer pressure, both positive and negative, compared to those in individualistic cultures. However, it is important to note that peer influence is not inherently negative. In fact, it can provide valuable social support and help teenagers develop important life skills.

In individualistic cultures, peer influence also plays a significant role, but the nature of this influence may differ. Adolescents in these cultures may prioritize personal achievement and independence, leading to different patterns of peer interaction and support. Understanding these cultural variations can help parents and educators develop strategies to support positive peer influence and mitigate negative behaviors.

Contrary to some beliefs, negative peer influence is not more prevalent in Eastern collectivistic cultures than in Western individualistic ones. Both types of cultures experience peer pressure, but the context and dynamics differ. In collectivistic cultures, the need for emotional support from peers may be less pronounced compared to individualistic cultures, where close peer relationships often play a critical role in emotional development.

Overall, peer influence is a complex and multifaceted aspect of adolescent development. Parents and educators should recognize the importance of peer relationships and work to support healthy interactions that contribute to teenagers' growth and well-being.

CHAPTER 19

Parenting and Cultural Identity

Cultural identity plays a vital role in shaping parenting practices, setting social expectations, and guiding behavior. For immigrant and refugee families, maintaining cultural connections while adapting to a new environment can be challenging but crucial for their children's development and well-being.

Preserving Cultural Heritage

Enhancing self-worth while simultaneously developing pride in one's cultural background is a complex task faced by parents worldwide. Each belief system, along with its traditions and customs, helps guide a child in developing a strong sense of individual identity and resilience. By examining child-rearing practices in countries such as Russia, Austria, Ghana, and Japan, we can see how distinct cultural beliefs, traditions, and expectations contribute to this process.

For example:

- **Russia**: Emphasizes strong family bonds and communal values, instilling a sense of belonging and collective identity.

- **Austria**: Values independence and self-reliance, encouraging children to explore their interests and develop autonomy.
- **Ghana**: Focuses on respect for elders and community cohesion, teaching children the importance of social harmony and mutual support.
- **Japan**: Prioritizes discipline and respect, fostering a sense of duty and responsibility towards family and society.

Parents strive to provide a sense of security for their children, teaching them to be proud of their heritage while developing self-worth and confidence. Despite the diverse paths taken by parents across cultures, the common goal remains the same: raising happy, well-adjusted, and productive adults.

Navigating Multiple Identities

Children of immigrant and refugee families often navigate multiple cultural identities, which can be both enriching and challenging. Supporting language acquisition, familiarizing children with diverse worldviews, and embracing diversity are essential strategies for helping children manage these multiple identities.

Expert advice on international rearing emphasizes the importance of positive reinforcement and creating a sense of worth. Involving the wider family in child-rearing and fostering empathy and freedom are also critical components. For instance, middle-class educated mothers may resonate more with family-focused advice, while an apolitical approach inspired by sociopolitical views can also be effective in teaching children to bridge cultural and social differences.

Navigating multiple identities can be a constant effort, as noted by Lutz Niethammer, leading to potential conflict and exhaustion. The political and cultural dimensions of identity mean that individuals' identities will never be entirely equal and harmonious. This complexity requires a nuanced understanding and approach to support children in developing a cohesive sense of self.

Cultural Assets and Positive Parenting

Preserving cultural heritage and emphasizing cultural assets are crucial for positive parenting in diverse populations. Immigrant and refugee families bring rich cultural traditions and values that can enhance their children's development. Policies and support structures should aim to reinforce these cultural assets while addressing negative or prejudicial practices.

For example, cultural research indicates that developing a sense of self is not an automatic process but a complex negotiation influenced by the broader social-cultural context. Family migrants draw from their cultural values, intentions, and necessities to understand the world, raise their children, and navigate new environments. Supporting these cultural connections helps families maintain their identity while adapting to a new society.

Overall, understanding and respecting cultural diversity in parenting practices can foster mutual understanding and emotional connections between individuals from different backgrounds. By celebrating cultural heritage and supporting positive parenting practices, we can create a more inclusive and supportive environment for all families.

CHAPTER 20

Parenting and Work-Life Balance

Balancing work and family life is a significant challenge for parents worldwide. This chapter examines the various policies and cultural beliefs that influence work-family conflict, the impact of maternity and paternity leave, and the role of flexible working arrangements.

Maternity and Paternity Leave

Maternity and paternity leave policies vary significantly across countries and have a profound impact on work-life balance for parents. In many Western nations, family policies aim to reduce work-family conflict by offering paid parental leave, subsidized childcare, and flexible work hours. However, the effectiveness of these policies can be influenced by broader cultural beliefs regarding gender roles and parenting responsibilities.

For example, the United States is unique among developed nations in not having mandated paid leave for new mothers, whereas 98 other countries offer paid breastfeeding breaks. Countries like Iraq provide new mothers with 72 days of paid leave, while Slovakia offers families $9,000 for their first child. In Brazil, mothers receive financial support during pregnancy, and Mexico allows parents to share up to six months of unpaid leave for child care.

The history of parental leave policies in France illustrates how political and social movements can shape child-rearing practices. The introduction of paid maternity leave in 1935 and the subsequent institutionalization of child care reflect the influence of the Communist parties and the women's movement. Similar trends can be seen in post-Communist European countries, where social health care and labor market programs have been integrated into work-family policies.

Flexible Working Arrangements

Flexible working arrangements are crucial for helping parents manage their dual responsibilities of work and family. Despite the increase in women's participation in the labor force, many households have both parents working full-time jobs. Research indicates that flexible work arrangements, such as part-time work or remote work, can significantly reduce work-family conflict and improve family well-being.

In the United States, women are more likely to work full-time than men, yet they also spend more time on child care and housework. This dual burden highlights the need for flexible working arrangements that accommodate the diverse needs of families. For example, when one spouse loses a job or a child experiences a medical emergency, the ability to adjust work schedules can alleviate stress and support family cohesion.

Employers and policymakers should consider the varying characteristics of individuals and family circumstances when designing work arrangements. Providing options for flexible hours, remote work, and job-sharing can help parents balance their professional and personal responsibilities more effectively.

Cultural Beliefs and Work-Family Conflict

Cultural beliefs about gender roles and parenting responsibilities play a significant role in shaping work-family conflict. Youth learn about these roles and expectations from an early age, influencing how they perceive and manage work and family life as adults. For instance, in Japan, Sweden, and the United States, work-family conflict is reported to be higher due to the pressure on parents to fulfill both work and family obligations.

Research from the International Social Survey Programme highlights the importance of addressing cultural norms to reduce work-family conflict. In some cultures, traditional gender roles may hinder efforts to achieve a balance between work and family. Encouraging more equitable sharing of responsibilities between mothers and fathers can help alleviate these pressures and promote a healthier work-life balance.

Global Perspectives on Work-Life Balance

Different countries have adopted various approaches to support work-life balance for parents. For example:

- **France**: Institutionalized child care and comprehensive family policies support working parents.
- **Brazil**: Financial support during pregnancy and flexible leave policies help mothers manage work and family responsibilities.
- **Mexico**: Shared parental leave policies allow both parents to participate in child care.

These examples demonstrate that effective work-life balance policies require a combination of legislative support, cultural change, and practical solutions that cater to the diverse needs of families.

CHAPTER 21

Parenting and Single Parenthood

Single parenthood is a significant aspect of modern family structures, particularly in countries like the United States, which has the highest proportion of single-parent households in the Western world. This chapter explores the challenges faced by single parents, the support systems available, and the approaches to co-parenting and shared custody.

Challenges and Support Systems

Parenting as a single parent presents unique challenges. Raising a child involves much more than providing basic needs; it requires navigating complex emotional, psychological, and social interactions. Single parents often bear the full responsibility of these tasks, which can be overwhelming.

In the United States, 18 million children under the age of 18 live in single-parent homes. This situation is prevalent across various social demographics, with significant percentages in black, Hispanic, and white families. Children in single-mother households are at a higher risk of experiencing poverty, highlighting the need for robust support systems.

Effective parenting support requires a structured, normative framework that offers emotional and psychological support. Society must provide a continuous plan execution, underlined by group approaches to capital investment, healthy capital, and social structures. This comprehensive support helps single parents manage the intricacies of child-rearing and ensures the well-being of both parents and children.

Co-Parenting and Shared Custody

Co-parenting and shared custody arrangements can alleviate some of the pressures faced by single parents. In countries like Canada, shared custody is common, allowing children to live with each parent on an alternating basis. This arrangement ensures that children benefit from the love and attention of both parents and reduces the pressure on any one parent.

For example, in Quebec, children often live with each parent weekly, benefiting from the involvement of both parents. In Australia, shared parenting post-separation is implemented under specific circumstances, ensuring that the child's best interests are prioritized.

Other custody arrangements include 75/25 and 60/40 splits, where one parent has the children for a larger portion of the time. In cases where parents cannot agree on a custody plan, a judge may appoint a Parenting Coordinator to mediate and make necessary adjustments to the plan.

In situations involving domestic violence, neglect, or abuse, an Order of Protection may be filed to restrict contact between the abuser and the abused, ensuring the safety and well-being of the children.

Legal and Social Implications

Legal and social implications play a crucial role in determining custody arrangements and supporting single parents. Many countries have laws that encourage co-parenting and shared custody, focusing on the best interests of the children. In the United States, there is no presumption for either type of custody, allowing for various forms of custody to be pursued through the judicial system.

Sole custody involves the child residing with one parent, while the other parent receives parenting time. Joint custody allows children to stay with both parents, often on a week-to-week basis. Each arrangement has its advantages and challenges, and the choice depends on the specific needs and circumstances of the family.

Overall, supporting single parents and promoting effective co-parenting and shared custody arrangements are essential for the well-being of children and the stability of families. By addressing the unique challenges faced by single parents and providing comprehensive support systems, society can help ensure positive outcomes for all family members.

CHAPTER 22

Parenting and Sibling Relationships

Sibling relationships play a crucial role in child development, influencing cognitive, social, and emotional growth. This chapter explores the dynamics of sibling relationships, the impact of birth order, and the prevalence and management of sibling rivalry across cultures.

Birth Order

Birth order has long been a topic of interest in both popular and scientific discourse. It is believed to influence personality traits and intelligence, with firstborns often perceived as more dominant, conscientious, and intelligent compared to their younger siblings. However, the evidence is mixed.

A study of 250,000 Norwegian conscripts found that firstborns, particularly males, had a statistically significant advantage in IQ relative to their younger siblings. However, other studies, such as those by Petter Kristensen and Tor Bjerkedal, have found that firstborns scored lower on various tests at 18 years of age compared to their siblings, after controlling for parental IQ and other confounding factors.

Popular stereotypes about birth order persist:

- **Firstborns**: Often seen as bossy, dominant, conscientious, and smarter, at least until the birth of a younger sibling.
- **Middle Children**: Perceived as neglected, social, manipulative, and rebellious, feeling caught between the rights of the firstborn and the indulgences of later children.
- **Youngest Children**: Known as the "babies" of the family, often viewed as charming troublemakers and the slothful mascots of the family.

Despite these stereotypes, research has shown that birth order is not a reliable predictor of personality traits. Studies across different cultures reveal that while birth order can influence certain behaviors, its impact varies widely and is often outweighed by other factors such as parenting style and family dynamics.

Sibling Rivalry

Sibling rivalry is a common and normal part of growing up, but it can also be problematic if not managed properly. Conflicts between siblings can arise due to competition for parental attention, differences in personality, and developmental stages.

In diverse cultures, sibling relationships can be both conflictual and supportive. For example, among the Himba of northern Namibia, older sisters help babies learn to walk, demonstrating a nurturing aspect of sibling relationships. In St. Lucia, toddlers model prosocial behavior from their mothers when helping parents with tasks, highlighting the importance of siblings in social and cognitive development.

Research has shown that children across the world want siblings to help them achieve important developmental goals, even when their relationships are conflictual. This mutual support and protection within families contribute to the overall well-being and development of children.

Managing sibling rivalry requires understanding its root causes and fostering positive interactions between siblings. Parents can encourage cooperation, set clear expectations for behavior, and provide equal attention to each child. By creating a supportive environment, parents can help reduce rivalry and promote healthy sibling relationships.

Cultural Perspectives on Sibling Relationships

Sibling relationships and rivalry can vary significantly across cultures. In some cultures, large family sizes and communal living arrangements foster close bonds between siblings. For example, in many African and Asian cultures, older siblings often take on caregiving roles, helping to raise younger siblings and contributing to household responsibilities.

In contrast, Western cultures may place a greater emphasis on individualism, leading to different dynamics in sibling relationships. However, the core principles of mutual support, protection, and cooperation remain relevant across all cultures.

Understanding these cultural differences can provide valuable insights into managing sibling relationships and promoting positive interactions. By acknowledging the unique context of each family, parents can adopt strategies that align with their cultural values and support their children's development.

CHAPTER 23

Parenting and Emotional Intelligence

Emotional intelligence (EI) is a crucial component of child development, influencing how individuals understand and manage their emotions and interact with others. This chapter explores the concept of emotional intelligence, the importance of teaching emotional skills, and the role of emotional regulation.

Teaching Emotional Skills

Teaching emotional skills is a fundamental aspect of parenting across cultures. Emotional intelligence helps individuals avoid negative emotional states and capitalize on positive emotions. American psychologist Daniel Goleman popularized the notion that high EI can significantly improve personal and professional success.

Emotional intelligence theories can be categorized into several models:

- **Trait Model**: EI is viewed as a constellation of stable traits.
- **Ability Model**: EI is seen as a set of mental abilities.
- **Mixture Model**: Combines traits and abilities.
- **Subjective Experience Model**: EI relates to the subjective experience of emotion.

While some research found little relation between EI and variables like leadership or managerial success, other studies have shown its relevance in non-relational jobs, such as writing and design.

Parents around the world recognize the importance of teaching emotional skills. Even in traditionally collectivist cultures like South Korea and Japan, emotional skills are highly valued. South Korean and Japanese parents prioritize self-discipline and restraint, while German-speaking parents emphasize emotional expression. These cultural differences reflect varying approaches to emotional education but underline the shared goal of fostering emotional intelligence in children.

Emotional Regulation

Emotional regulation is the ability to manage and respond to emotional experiences effectively. It is a critical aspect of emotional intelligence and significantly impacts children's development.

Media, particularly children's television programs, play a role in shaping children's understanding of emotions. American television programs often depict happy emotional climates, with negative emotions quickly resolved. This raises concerns about what children learn from these portrayals, as they may develop unrealistic expectations about emotions.

Different cultural approaches to emotional regulation are evident. Chinese parents, for example, are less likely to encourage emotional expression compared to American parents. Chinese mothers often teach children to suppress negative emotions, while American parents, particularly fathers, endorse comforting behaviors when children display negative emotions.

Studies comparing Chinese and British youths found that British students were more aware of strategies used by Chinese students to mask emotions. Similarly, Taiwanese middle school students noticed the American tendency to express rather than hide emotions. These differences highlight the cultural variability in teaching emotional regulation.

Understanding and respecting these cultural differences is essential for effective emotional education. By providing children with tools to manage their emotions, parents can help them navigate social interactions and develop resilience.

Importance of Emotional Intelligence

Emotional intelligence is vital for personal and social success. High EI individuals are better equipped to handle stress, build healthy relationships, and achieve their goals. Teaching children emotional skills and regulation strategies sets the foundation for a well-adjusted and fulfilling life.

Parents play a crucial role in fostering emotional intelligence. By modeling emotional regulation, providing support, and encouraging open communication, parents can help their children develop strong emotional skills. This, in turn, promotes positive mental health and overall well-being.

CHAPTER 24

Parenting and Special Needs

Parenting children with special needs presents unique challenges and opportunities. This chapter explores the perceptions of disabilities, the impact of Autism Spectrum Disorder (ASD), and the cultural perspectives on learning disabilities.

Autism Spectrum Disorder

Autism Spectrum Disorder (ASD) is characterized by persistent deficits in social communication and interaction, along with restricted, repetitive patterns of behavior. Historically, ASD has been viewed as a predominantly Western "cultural affliction," often equated with "mental retardation." However, recent research has shifted this perspective.

Consensus findings from the Consortium of Psychiatric Epidemiology Studies indicate a decrease in the prevalence of lifetime mental retardation and learning disabilities in childhood. Studies in diverse cultural settings, such as India, have identified developmental milestones and familial characteristics of autism, highlighting the variability in how ASD is recognized and managed.

The Diagnostic and Statistical Manual of Mental Disorders (DSM-5) emphasizes the importance of examining each individual's developmental history and co-morbid conditions when diagnosing ASD. Early intervention and comprehensive assessments are crucial for supporting children with ASD and helping them achieve their full potential.

Learning Disabilities

Learning disabilities, once considered a predominantly Western issue, are now recognized worldwide. The identification and description of learning disabilities vary across cultures, with Eastern cultures historically lacking a concept for these traits.

Ethnographic approaches, combining focused interviews and participant observation, have been used to study learning disabilities in diverse cultural contexts. For example, in China, there has been an increasing awareness of learning disabilities, prompting discussions and interventions tailored to the cultural context.

The phrase "Meeting the challenges of Learning Disabilities internationally" encapsulates the goal of understanding and addressing learning disabilities in various countries. By combining insights from Western and Eastern perspectives, researchers aim to create a more inclusive and effective approach to supporting individuals with learning disabilities.

Perceptions and Support for Special Needs

Parental perspectives on disabilities significantly influence how children with special needs are treated and supported. In some cultures, children with disabilities are integrated into the community and treated similarly to their typically developing peers, leading to remarkable achievements. For example, Polish students with disabilities often speak multiple languages and participate fully in society.

In contrast, in other cultures, children with disabilities may be sheltered and less visible in the community, resulting in fewer opportunities for integration and development. Changing these perceptions requires open, public discussions about the abilities and potential of individuals with disabilities.

Parents play a crucial role in advocating for their children and ensuring they receive the support they need. Educating parents about the capabilities of children with special needs and fostering an inclusive environment can help these children thrive.

Overall, understanding and respecting cultural differences in perceptions of disabilities and providing targeted support can significantly improve the lives of children with special needs and their families.

CHAPTER 25

Parenting and Peer Relationships

Peer relationships play a vital role in children's social and emotional development. This chapter explores how everyday peer experiences influence parent-child dynamics, friendships, social skills, and the impact of bullying and peer pressure.

Friendships and Social Skills

Friendships are essential for children's development, providing opportunities for learning social skills, empathy, and cooperation. As children grow, their reliance on peer relationships increases, and these interactions significantly shape their behavior and emotional well-being.

As a parent, understanding the importance of early childhood friendships can help you support your child's social development. Encouraging positive interactions, teaching empathy, and providing opportunities for socialization are crucial steps in helping children navigate their relationships. For instance, schools in Finland and Italy are viewed as peaceful places that foster growth and active involvement, highlighting the role of educational environments in supporting children's social development.

Research indicates that a strong majority of parents in various countries are satisfied with their children's schools, appreciating the nurturing and inspiring environments they provide. By fostering a positive atmosphere at home and encouraging healthy friendships, parents can help their children build meaningful and fulfilling relationships.

Bullying and Peer Pressure

Bullying and peer pressure are significant challenges that children and adolescents face. These negative peer experiences can have lasting effects on a child's mental health and self-esteem. Understanding the dynamics of bullying and peer pressure is essential for parents to provide appropriate support and intervention.

A study involving over 200,000 children in 40 countries revealed that "resilience" is a universal strength. Resilience refers to a child's ability to approach problems confidently and consider options when problem-solving. A resilient child possesses strong intrinsic skills, including self-regulation and social skills, which are crucial for navigating peer pressure and bullying.

Interestingly, children's responses to bullying and peer pressure vary across cultures. For example, 85% of children in India reported feeling sorry for peers being bullied, indicating a high level of empathy. In contrast, children from Japan, Kenya, and South Korea showed lower response rates to peer consideration questions. These variations highlight the importance of cultural context in understanding and addressing peer-related challenges.

Parents can play a pivotal role in fostering resilience and helping children cope with bullying and peer pressure. Encouraging open communication, teaching problem-solving skills, and promoting empathy can empower children to handle difficult peer interactions effectively.

Impact on Parent-Child Relationships

Everyday peer experiences significantly impact parent-child relationships. As children spend a considerable amount of time with their peers, their social circumstances and interactions influence their behavior, emotions, and identity. The quality of these relationships can affect the connections between parents and children, shaping the overall family dynamic.

Parents should be aware of their children's peer experiences and provide support when needed. Engaging in conversations about friendships, bullying, and peer pressure can help parents understand their children's social world and offer guidance. Additionally, fostering a positive family environment that values open communication and mutual respect can strengthen parent-child bonds and support children's social and emotional development.

Understanding the interplay between peer relationships and family dynamics is crucial for parents to create a nurturing and supportive environment. By recognizing the importance of peer experiences and addressing any challenges that arise, parents can help their children develop healthy relationships and thrive both socially and emotionally.

CHAPTER 26

Parenting and Divorce

Divorce can significantly impact both parents and children, affecting their well-being and relationships. This chapter explores the processes and dynamics of parenting after divorce, co-parenting practices, and the impact on children's well-being.

Co-Parenting after Divorce

Co-parenting after divorce is crucial for maintaining a stable environment for children. Effective co-parenting requires collaboration and communication between both parents, ensuring that the child's needs are prioritized.

In Hungary, data from the National Office for the Judiciary indicates that most parents with child support agreements keep their children every second weekend. This trend reflects the challenges of maintaining contact with older children, who may have different needs and schedules. Court decisions often follow this pattern, with older children spending weekends with the non-custodial parent.

Scandinavian countries, known for their child-centered practices, emphasize the importance of co-parenting. Despite the challenges, the goal is to ensure that both parents remain actively involved in their children's lives. In 2011, less than 14% of children under 18 in Scandinavia received equal or more than 40% of visits by the non-custodial parent, highlighting the need for improved practices to support co-parenting.

In assessing the impact of divorce on children, it is essential to consider the role of co-parenting in promoting well-being. Voluntary agreements on child support, visitation, and living arrangements can help create a more stable and supportive environment for children post-divorce.

Impact on Children's Well-being

Divorce can have varying effects on children's well-being, influenced by factors such as conflict levels, parental involvement, and cultural norms. Research indicates that children experiencing low to high conflict dynamics after their parents' divorce have worse outcomes than those in stable high- or low-conflict families.

In the United States, children report higher life satisfaction compared to their peers in other countries. This may be attributed to greater perceived autonomy and opportunities for engagement in extracurricular activities. However, these children are less well-rated by their peers, suggesting that social competence and peer relationships play a significant role in their overall well-being.

Children's well-being is closely linked to their perceptions of control and mastery. Providing children with choices and opportunities for self-reliance can enhance their sense of satisfaction and competence. Additionally, fostering positive peer relationships and social skills is crucial for their emotional and social development.

Cultural Perspectives on Divorce and Parenting

Cultural norms and policies significantly influence how divorce and parenting are approached in different countries. For example, American culture ingrains specific behaviors and expectations, while Norwegian policies and cultural norms produce distinct parenting practices.

When research from one culture is applied to another context, variations in processes and outcomes may emerge. Studying the transition from low to high conflict in divorced parents' relationships, researchers found similar patterns in Norway and the U.S., with elevated conflict predicting worse child outcomes. These findings underscore the universal challenges of divorce and the need for context-specific interventions.

Overall, understanding the cultural, legal, and social factors that shape parenting after divorce is essential for supporting families through this transition. By fostering effective co-parenting practices, promoting children's well-being, and addressing cultural differences, we can help mitigate the negative impacts of divorce on families.

CHAPTER 27

Parenting and Safety

Parenting decisions related to safety vary significantly across cultures and environments. The physical environment, local laws, and cultural attitudes all play crucial roles in shaping how parents protect and guide their children.

Childproofing the Home

Childproofing is a common practice among American parents to ensure the safety of their children within the home. This involves installing safety gates, securing furniture, and using childproof locks on cabinets. In contrast, in Japan, childproofing is virtually nonexistent. Japanese parents often rely on teaching children to avoid hazards rather than physically altering the environment.

For example, my son and his neighborhood playmates were walking out the brightly painted front door when I hastily stopped them, pointing out dangers like pollution and traffic. Japanese parents, however, often feel less concern about such dangers, reflecting a cultural difference in safety practices. This lack of emphasis on security appears interesting, especially in a highly urbanized society like Japan.

While American parents might feel compelled to create a childproof environment, Japanese parents trust their children to learn and navigate potential dangers. This difference highlights how cultural attitudes influence parenting practices.

Stranger Danger

"Stranger danger" is a concept that varies widely between cultures. In the United States, fear of strangers is a significant concern, leading to an emphasis on teaching children to avoid unknown individuals. This concept defines intergenerational mistrust and influences parenting decisions.

In Japan, the rhetoric around "stranger danger" is much less prevalent. The low crime rate and educational emphasis on communal responsibility contribute to a sense of safety. Japanese parents often teach their children not to fear people and to seek help from others when needed. This communal approach fosters a sense of trust and security among children.

Studies have shown that Japanese children demonstrate less fear of strangers compared to their Western counterparts. This difference can be attributed to cultural values regarding age and kinship, as well as the low crime rates in Japan. In contrast, British and American children may develop an impressionable fear of strangers due to the messages they receive from society and media.

Environmental Influences on Safety

The physical environment significantly impacts children's safety and parenting decisions. Factors such as the number of playgrounds, the type of schools, and the safety of streets influence how parents protect their children. Recommendations and policies related to safety vary greatly from one society to another.

For example, truancy laws differ between countries, with Australia treating it as a serious crime and Montenegro having no legal punishment. Similarly, seat belt and car seat laws are stricter in the United States than in Spain or Portugal, where rear-seat passenger seat belts are not legally required for people over the age of 15.

The Grimms, American parents living in Ghent, Belgium, noted that the safety of the streets and lack of law enforcement at playgrounds influenced their parenting decisions. They allowed their five-year-old to bike alone, a decision they might not have made in Chicago. This example illustrates how living in a different environment can change parents' criteria for safety and the rules they implement for their children.

Understanding these differences can help parents navigate safety concerns and make informed decisions based on their environment and cultural context. By considering both local practices and cultural values, parents can create a safe and supportive environment for their children.

CHAPTER 28

Parenting and Cultural Values

Cultural values deeply influence parenting practices and the development of children. This chapter explores the differences between individualistic and collectivist cultures, the emphasis on respect and obedience, and the value placed on independence and individuality.

Respect and Obedience

In many cultures, respect and obedience are central values in child-rearing. For example, traditional Indian ethics emphasize the duty to respect and obey one's elders, including parents, guests, and teachers. Children are taught to show humility, attend to adults, and follow moral precepts outlined in texts like the Manusmṛti. This perspective reflects the broader cultural milieu that values deference to adult views and decisions.

Respect and obedience are not limited to Indian culture. Many collectivist cultures prioritize social cohesion and interpersonal relationships, discouraging direct assertions of the self. Children in these cultures are often encouraged to prioritize group harmony and respect for authority.

Independence and Individuality

In contrast, individualistic cultures, such as those in the United States, Canada, and Northern Europe, emphasize independence and autonomy. Parents in these cultures often encourage children to develop their own identities and make independent decisions. Language techniques like praise are used to facilitate this development.

For instance, in Germany, it is uncommon for grandparents to take on hands-on tasks of caring for and cleaning kids, reflecting a cultural value of self-reliance. In Scandinavia, independence is highly valued, and it would be considered unusual for parents to rely heavily on extended family for child-rearing support.

Mothers in these cultures may leave the hospital shortly after childbirth and use practical solutions like the Tübingen box, a custom-made cardboard box with a mattress for infants. This practice highlights the cultural emphasis on practicality and self-sufficiency.

Cultural Differences in Parenting Beliefs

The differences in parenting beliefs between individualistic and collectivist cultures are significant. Western cultures tend to conceptualize the self as independent and autonomous, while East Asian cultures see the self as socially embedded or interdependent. These contrasting views shape parenting practices and the development of children.

For example, caregivers in individualistic societies pay heightened attention to the autonomy of the child, allowing more free play and self-initiated exploration. This approach is believed to foster overall developmental paths. In contrast, collectivist cultures focus on maintaining social cohesion and discourage behaviors that assert the self over the group.

These cultural values influence not only parenting practices but also how children perceive themselves and interact with others. Understanding these differences can help parents navigate the complexities of raising children in diverse cultural contexts.

CHAPTER 29

Parenting and Adoption

Adoption is a deeply impactful and complex aspect of parenting, influenced by cultural, legal, and social factors. This chapter explores the processes and challenges of international and transracial adoption, emphasizing the importance of meeting the needs of both parents and children.

International Adoption

International adoption involves placing a child with adoptive parents across national borders, raising various ethical and practical concerns. The history, theoretical concerns, and research findings in international adoption highlight the complexities of this practice. For example, a 2015 law made international adoption more difficult, yet countries like China and Russia hosted significantly more children with US adoptive families in 2016 compared to 2015.

International adoption aims to meet the needs of both parents and children, offering a unique path to parenthood. However, it also raises questions about identity, cultural integration, and the well-being of the child. An estimated two million children live with a different nationality than their parents, illustrating the global scale of international adoption.

Countries describe international adoption as the best choice for children in need of families, but concerns about its practice persist.

Ethical considerations, such as the child's right to maintain their cultural heritage and the potential for exploitation, remain critical issues. Families and policymakers must navigate these challenges to ensure the best outcomes for adopted children.

Transracial Adoption

Transracial adoption occurs when adoptive parents and children come from different racial or ethnic backgrounds. This practice brings unique challenges and opportunities for fostering racial and cultural diversity within families.

Evaluating both negative and positive aspects of a transracial adoptive environment is essential for guiding future practice, policy, and research. Negative aspects include racial and ethnic discrimination, while positive aspects encompass the value of racial and cultural diversity and affiliation with one's background.

Three conceptual frameworks assist in understanding transracial adoption:

1. **Community Resilience Model**: Provides parameters for evaluating global group well-being.
2. **Fosterage Concept**: Introduces multivalent conceptualizations of racial and ethnic identity, moving beyond mainstream either/or approaches.
3. **Post-Racial Perspective**: Considers resilient but non-fixed racial identity issues in the United States.

In the USA, 90 to 95 percent of adoptive children are matched with adoptive parents of the same race, while only 22 to 25 percent of international adoptions involve same-race matches. This statistic highlights the cultural diversity inherent in international adoptive families.

Transracial adoption provides a unique opportunity to compare the impact of nature versus nurture, especially in attachment and intelligence. By embracing the complexities of racial and ethnic identity, adoptive families can foster an environment that values diversity and resilience.

Cultural Differences in Adoption Practices

Adoption policies and practices vary widely across countries, influenced by religious, legislative, and societal factors. Some countries promote high numbers of adoptions, while others prioritize domestic adoptions to preserve cultural and linguistic continuity. Expatriates often face challenges when adopting in their country of residence, highlighting the need for a nuanced understanding of local adoption policies.

Understanding these cultural differences is crucial for adoptive families and policymakers. By respecting the cultural heritage of adopted children and ensuring ethical practices, families can create supportive and inclusive environments for their children.

CHAPTER 30

Parenting and Grandparenting

Grandparents play a crucial role in the lives of their grandchildren, and their involvement can vary significantly across cultures. This chapter explores the roles of grandparents, the benefits of their involvement, and the dynamics of intergenerational relationships.

Role of Grandparents

Grandparents often provide valuable support in child-rearing, especially in cultures with strong intergenerational ties. Their involvement can help maintain traditional cultural values, especially in immigrant families where parents may have assimilated to new cultures.

Among the Minangkabau of Indonesia, grandparents of both the mother and father are expected to care for the child, emphasizing the saying, "the grandparent's love is heavier [than the parent's]." In many indigenous cultures, grandparents live within the same community as their grandchildren, allowing for frequent contact and the transmission of traditional knowledge. For example, the Asdzaan Apache grandmother shares information with her granddaughter, highlighting the importance of close contact.

In contrast, in contemporary societies, weakened family ties have led to less frequent contact between grandparents and grandchildren. However, cross-cultural studies have shown the potential benefits of grandparental involvement, such as higher life satisfaction and reduced loneliness for grandparents.

Different cultures emphasize the role of grandparents in various ways. For example, the Hmong and Mien recognize the role of grandparents in the nuclear family, with the Mien assigning the most important grandparent role to maternal grandparents. Other groups, such as Japanese, Chinese, Korean, Ethiopian, Indian, Mexican, Trinidadian, Cuban, Afro-Caribbean, English, Sierra Leonean, Pakistani, Ghanaian, Brazilian, and Turkish, also highlight the helpfulness of grandparents in rearing children.

Intergenerational Relationships

Intergenerational relationships undergo significant shifts as communities evolve. The disengagement theory suggests that older adults withdraw from society, while the socio-emotional selectivity theory argues that older adults are highly invested in relationships with their extended family.

Modernization theory posits that internal migration and urbanization weaken respect for and interest in older adults. Data from various societies support this claim, showing that less modernized communities demonstrate favoritism for the aged, with older adults participating as central figures within their communities. These older adults are seen as repositories of culture and tradition, offering emotional connections to the past and meaning for the future.

Promoting positive intergenerational relations involves understanding the factors that influence the relationship between grandchildren and grandparents. The Social Mirror model outlines three general shifts:

1. **Focus on the Future**: Young individuals prepare for limitless futures by defining themselves through their goals and aspirations.
2. **Reflection on Life**: As people age, they reflect on their lives as a whole, focusing on their legacy and self-worth through past efforts.
3. **Appreciation for the Past**: Older adults are valued for their cultural knowledge and emotional connections to the past, contributing to the overall well-being of their communities.

By fostering these shifts, societies can promote positive intergenerational relationships and ensure that the valuable contributions of older adults are recognized and appreciated.

CHAPTER 31

Parenting and Emotional Well-being

The emotional well-being of both parents and children is critical for healthy development and family dynamics. This chapter explores the historical context of parenting, the importance of self-care for parents, and the concept of parental burnout.

Self-Care for Parents

Self-care for parents is a crucial aspect of effective parenting. Parents who manage their stress levels can model healthy self-regulation for their children, which is essential for their cognitive, emotional, social, and academic development. A meta-analytical study from 2008 found that children of stressed caretakers displayed more behavioral problems and lower cognitive performance.

Parents who invest time in caring for themselves can maintain emotional availability and resilience, providing secure attachments and reducing negative effects on their children. This reciprocal relationship between parent and child fosters an environment where children can learn to process emotions and regulate their behavior effectively.

Effective parenting requires parents to manage societal expectations and the challenges of raising children experiencing emotional and physical changes. By prioritizing their well-being, parents can better support their children's development and overall emotional health.

Parental Burnout

Parental burnout is a phenomenon similar to occupational burnout but specific to parenting. It includes exhaustion, emotional distancing from one's children, and a sense of incompetence. Research has shown that parental burnout is more common among mothers than fathers, particularly when caring for children with conditions like Autism Spectrum Disorder (ASD).

Parents of children with ASD often experience high levels of stress due to the child's symptoms, which can bring psychological distress to the family. Coping strategies for parental burnout include distancing, escape, and acceptance of the child's imperfections. These strategies help parents manage the burden and maintain their well-being.

Understanding and addressing parental burnout is essential for supporting parents and ensuring they can provide the necessary care and support for their children. Future research on parental burnout should consider factors such as contributing elements, core dimensions, and family-level signs of burnout.

Historical Context of Parenting

Historically, parenting approaches have evolved from strict discipline to more affectionate and supportive methods. In the 19th century, psychological treatises emphasized not spoiling children and advocated for discipline and punishment for misbehavior. Influential Christian writers like Palladius suggested that strict parenting could help children develop inner strength and wisdom.

As societal and economic norms shifted towards white-collar occupations and academic success, the emphasis on parenting extended beyond survival and thriving. Today, the relationship between parental support and children's well-being is well-researched, highlighting the importance of responsiveness, effort, and positive interactions.

By understanding the historical context and current research on parenting, parents can adopt effective strategies that promote their emotional well-being and support their children's development.